Family Bucket Lists

Bring More Fun, Adventure & Camaraderie Into Every Day

Lara Krupicka

Family Bucket Lists
Copyright © 2013 Lara Krupicka

Cover image by Alexander Raths

Wordcrafter Communications

1119 Sara Ln., Naperville, IL 60565

Visit the website at: www.larakrupicka.com

ISBN: 0615879772

ISBN-13: 978-0615879772

1. Parenting & Relationships. 2. Parenting & Relationships— Family Activities. I. Title.

Table of Contents

Introduction:
The Bucket List Explained

We are the music makers...and we are the dreamers of dreams.
~ Willie Wonka and the Chocolate Factory

Have you ever reacted to hearing about an activity or vacation spot with the comment, "that's on my bucket list"? You probably weren't talking about a written list. You were simply voicing a hope, however deeply held and however serious your intentions were for completing it.

But the exciting news is: behind every bucket list wish resides the inspiration to make everyday life more adventurous. We just need to recapture the term "bucket list" in a way that transforms it from a wish to a regular practice that fits our family life.

Bucket List Defined

The term "bucket list" came into vogue only in the last decade, particularly after the 2007 release of the Rob Reiner film by that name (starring Jack Nicholson and Morgan Freeman as two cancer patients on the run from the hospital, trying to get in their last few adventures before they "kick the bucket").

Now bucket list is so much a part of our everyday language that it was officially added to the Merriam-Webster Dictionary in 2012:

bucket list:

a list of things that one has not done before but wants to do before dying.

When bucket lists come up in conversation they often include mentions of exotic vacations (seeing the pyramids in Egypt, climbing to the top of Machu Picchu, visiting Red Square in Moscow) or accomplishing great athletic feats (running a marathon, competing in the Olympics, scaling a mountain).

The typical concept of a bucket list puts it way out of reach for ordinary moms and everyday kids. Who has the time – to train, to travel, to experience these things? Who has the money for the airfare, the tour guides, the trainers? And frankly, what mom wants to risk her life or the lives of her kids for the sake of checking off some of the goals contained on these far out lists?

Despite this perception, bucket lists can be a powerful tool in the life of a family. They can be a tool yielding benefits beyond the experiences on the list. So it is time to redefine "bucket list" to include families and our needs.

Bucket Lists For Family Life

For our purposes, a bucket list is a compilation of dreams and aspirations that reflects the heart desires of the creator (or creators). A bucket list is a personal document, not a copycat of what others deem important. Your bucket list is what you value. After all, your desires look different from mine and your children's dreams do not necessarily match those of my children. Therefore, our bucket lists will be different from each other. Your children's lists will also be different from yours. In fact, you may be surprised to discover what people you know and love long to do, see, and experience in life.

Under this modified definition your bucket list can include both seemingly impossible intentions (be the youngest person to reach the South Pole) and short-term, ordinary-sounding goals (get on the honor roll for one semester).

Compiled under this framework, your bucket lists will foster a lifestyle mindset of enjoying the process. Progress toward completion of your dreams will matter as much as the realization of the dream itself, in contrast to the "one-and-done" attitude representative of stereotypical bucket lists.

Another form your bucket list can take is one comprised of life dreams you have already realized. This allows you to recognize and celebrate the dreams you have had the fortune to live out thus far. In turn this can motivate you and your family to keep making dreams happen.

And within our new definition you'll hopefully want to create a family bucket list that every family member helps devise, after each person has had a chance to work on an individual list. The family bucket list is a list that you work on fulfilling together. Rather than a list of what your family wants to do before dying, it will document intentions for the years your children live at home (although it is great to eventually continue the list into the college years and beyond).

Think about it: with this concept of a bucket list, you can be living a bucket list life in small ways each and every day. And why not? Why wait for the perfect timing or setting when you can grab hold of bucket list opportunities all along the way?

Put That In Writing

Research shows there is power in putting our goals (or dreams) into writing. According to David Kohl, professor emeritus at Virginia Tech:

- 80% of Americans claim they have no goals.

- 16% acknowledge that they do have goals but do not write them down.

- Less than 4% put their goals in writing and fewer than 1% review them on an ongoing basis.

Additionally, researcher Dr. Gail Matthews of Dominican University in California discovered that:

- Just writing down a goal, versus merely thinking of one, provided significantly greater success (between 33-50% more achieved).

- Writing down a goal and sharing it with a friend accomplished more than the act of writing it down alone.

- Writing down a goal, sharing it with a friend, and then checking in regularly about progress toward the goal elicited noticeably higher levels of achievement than writing and sharing the goal without regular accountability.

Written bucket lists, created in the supportive environment of family where lists are shared and reviewed often, harness all the power for success highlighted by these studies. So why not create your own bucket lists? Once each of you do, your entire family will be one step closer to living the life they had only dreamed about.

Creating Your Own Bucket List

Have you given yourself permission to dream? Good! Because you get to create your individual bucket list first — the one that represents your hopes, desires and goals. Create the list that is tailor-made for you and causes you to wake up excited each day. To do this, you need to dig deep and listen to what your heart tells you, even if what you hear makes you feel silly or vulnerable.

If you were asked to list right now what goes on your bucket list, you could probably give a handful of ideas. But those ideas only scratch the surface of your true desires. You might cite a few possibilities you have unintentionally lifted from other people's bucket list ideas. That is, they are ideas that sound exciting or glamorous, without making you enthusiastic at the core of who you are. And that is okay. But the more personal buy-in you have for each dream on your list, the more you will put in the effort in to make it happen. A well-fitted aspiration is more apt to energize you than frustrate you.

Creating your own bucket list should be fun, but it will also take some effort. A worthwhile list won't come together in a few minutes or an hour. But you can build it over the course of days or weeks. And remember, for a list to be motivating in a way that keeps you moving forward, it needs to be one that comes from inside of you – not from a premade list someone else brainstormed.

Thankfully, when you are willing to make the time for it, the art of creating your personal bucket list can be an adventure in itself. You will travel through time, tap into long-buried interests, and come out holding treasures. You are in for a thrill ride.

So go ahead and jot down any list items that come to mind right away. Consider also finding a method for capturing all of the ideas that spring to mind in the days to come, such as a sticky-note pad kept in a pocket or purse. Once you have your mind on your bucket list, you may recall old desires at odd moments. Don't lose those memories or moments of inspiration – they can feed some interesting possibilities for your list.

Once you've tapped the top-of-mind ideas proceed through the exercises that follow. Respond fully to every question, even if you have already accomplished a goal you had in your teens or currently face an insurmountable limitation to fulfilling a desire you once held. Write every idea down anyway. Think of each one as a clue to what you most desire.

Complete each portion of the individual questions – the What You Want to Do, What You Want to See, Who You Want to Be, and Who You Want to Meet portions – separately over the course of several days or weeks. You may find reading through all of the questions quickly the first time helps to get your mind turning. You'll still probably want to reread them, allowing some time between readings for memories and ideas to surface. This is both a soul-searching and a brainstorming exercise. Giving yourself time to unearth the answers will be better in the long run than rushing to compile your bucket list right away. Consider returning to the questions multiple times, seeing what new ideas have percolated to the surface of your memory as you prime the bucket list brainstorming engine.

In the upcoming pages, you will find separate questionnaires for parents and kids. Each set is intended to meet the creator at his or her level, with children's questions distinguished by age. Guide younger children through their list creation, but give older children space to be themselves and explore their hopes and dreams individually, without too much of your influence. Allow your teen, tween or older elementary child to answer the questions completely on his own. You will have a chance to share your answers with each other and hear what your child has discovered once each member of the family is ready to share his list.

Questions for Mom & Dad

In each of the following four rounds of questions, you are going to progress through time. First look back into your childhood and your earliest memories. Then examine those tumultuous teen years, and sift through your pre-kids adult life before finally wandering amongst your hopes from recent years. Have fun remembering what has captured your interest at different points in your life.

You may have more than one answer to each question or you may have a different answer each time you go through the questions, and this is totally fine. Just go with whatever ideas come up!

WHAT YOU WANT TO DO

What is on your bucket list of things you always wanted to DO? If anything comes immediately to mind write it down. If nothing comes to mind right away, do not panic. Steadily work your way through the questions. No doubt you will soon be jotting down more and more ideas.

Childhood dreams

Was there a skill, sport or physical feat you wanted to master as a child but never did? Was it due to lack of ability, lack of practice, lack of training, or some combination of these things? What is keeping you from trying to master it now?

In your childhood, was there an experience you hoped to have that never came to be? Is there someone you would have liked to go through a special experience with? If it is not possible to share this with them today, would taking part in the experience honor that person's memory in some way?

Was there a particular activity you wished you could have taken part in, but you were too young at the time? Would you like the chance to attempt it now?

Teen/Young Adult Aspirations

What event or experience would you have loved to be a part of at this time in your life?

Did you want to achieve something at this age, but did not make it? Does it matter that you are no longer a teen? Would you still want to achieve something similar now?

As a teenager/young adult you wanted to try [fill in the blank]. As an adult do you still want to try it?

Ambitions Before Kids

How would you have loved to spend free time before kids, if you had known what life would be like now?

Hopes in Recent Years

Has a new interest come up for you recently? Is there something you want to learn how to do or a hobby you would like to take up?

Is there an action you have put off taking recently, whether out of fear or for another reason? Does the idea keep hounding you?

How do you dream of spending your retirement years, in terms of activities or what you will be doing with your time?

WHAT YOU WANT TO SEE

Where would you like to go and what would you most like to see in your lifetime? List any top-of-mind ideas first, then progress to the questions below.

Childhood dreams

What place did you wish to go to most when you were a kid? Did you ever get there? If so, would it be worth returning to?

When you were young, what sort of place did you dream of living? Was it a particular location or type of home? Have you lived in a place like that since childhood? If not, is it a location or place where you could rent a home for a brief time to experience what it would be like?

Did you have a special location you liked to visit as a child? A vacation spot? Someone's house? What about that place made it so special? Have you been back there recently? Would you like to go there again in the future?

Teen/Young Adult Aspirations

What would have been your ideal "road trip" or spring break destination at this age? What made it ideal to you then? Would it still be ideal to you now?

Was there a group or performer you would have loved to have seen live on stage (whether a musical performance or theatre show), but did not get to?

Ambitions Before Kids

What was on your list of travel destinations during your adult years before kids?

Was there an artifact or artwork you would have loved to view up close, but missed?

Hopes in Recent Years

What is on your list of places to go now? How about once the kids are grown?

Is there a place you would like to visit on your own or with friends (but not with your family)?

What would your ideal night of entertainment be – where would you go, what would you see?

Is there a historical event coming up that you would like to witness?

WHO YOU WANT TO BE

What/who have you always wanted to be, whether it be a role you have wanted to fill or a character quality you have wanted to embody?

Childhood Dreams

Who were your idols as a child?

Did you play pretend or make believe as a child? If so, what role(s) did you most frequently assume?

When people asked you what you wanted to be when you grew up, what was your answer? Did the answer change over time? List as many roles as you can remember.

Teen/Young Adult Aspirations

Did you have a hero as a teen? What made you look up to them?

When you first entered high school (or even college), what career were you considering? What drew you to that type of work?

What job did you most want to get when you were interviewing for work? Was there a position you hoped your job would lead to?

Ambitions Before Kids

If you left work to be at home with your children, what trajectory was your career on when you left? Where might it have led? Where did you want it to lead?

If you stayed with your career while raising children, did you shift your ambitions to accommodate family life? Are there career aspirations that you have let drop for now that you might pick up again in the future?

Hopes in Recent Years

Have you considered a second career or change in career as your children become older? What would you like your career to look like?

If money, connections, experience, or talent, were no object, what would be your ideal job?

What kind of person will you want people to remember you as when you are gone?

WHO YOU WANT TO MEET

What person(s), living or dead, would you like to interact with, face to face, even briefly?

Childhood Dreams

Who did you hope to be like when you grew up?

What athlete, movie star, author, musician, dignitary, or other celebrity would you have loved to meet as a child? List as many names as you can remember (even if they are not still living).

Teen/Young Adult Aspirations

Name an individual (or group) you were crazy about as a teen.

Name an expert who inspired teenaged/young adult you. What did they do so well that impressed you?

Ambitions Before Kids

Is there a person who stands out in your memory as having influenced you from afar in your pre-kids years?

What celebrity who was popular before you had kids would you have liked to meet?

Hopes in Recent Years

Whose work or lifestyle have you admired from afar?

Is there someone whose opinion or way of thinking about things you would love to learn one-on-one?

Name one person you do not know well but think you would hit it off great with, if given a chance.

Questions for Teens and Tweens

Does your tween or teen already have a bucket list? I bet they have ideas of places they would like to go one day, people they would like to meet and things they would like to try. I bet they will be happy to learn that you are interested in not simply hearing about those dreams, but also being a part of helping them take place. Isn't this really something everyone longs to hear?

Have your teen/tween answer the following questions as honestly as possible. Encourage him or her to take ample time and reflect carefully on each question. Try giving your child one set of questions each day. Slow down if necessary. Encourage your tween/teen to embrace new ideas that strike seemingly out of nowhere. Suggest jotting down ideas on a scrap of paper and adding them to lists later. See if they would like a folder or box set aside to keep the scraps of ideas as they come in. Let your child know you are working through your own brainstorming exercises. Offer to share some of the ideas you are discovering from your list. When all the questions are completed, your child will come back and create a customized "bucket list."

WHAT YOU WANT TO DO

What is on your bucket list of things you always wanted to do? If anything comes immediately to mind, write it down.

Early Years Dreams

Thinking back to when you were a very young child, what was your favorite way to spend your playtime? What made it so enjoyable for you?

Was there something as a little kid that you always wished you could do, but were too young to do and never found a chance to do as you got older?

Grade School Hopes

Was there a sport or hobby you wanted to try when you were in grade school, but you were too shy to say so or you did not have the time or money for it?

At this age, did you have something you hoped to get good at, but you never received the help to learn better or did not have the dexterity or maturity you needed?

If you could go back to being your grade school self, what would you have done differently? How would you have spent your free time?

Was there a pet you wanted to own, or an animal you wanted to interact with?

Current Wishes

What would be the most awesome way to spend a free day, if you had the money to do anything?

In the coming years is there a new sport you would like to try, a new hobby you would like to learn or a club you would like to join?

If you were told you could not fail, what new thing would you try?

Future Ideas

Is there something you would like to do when you are older – as a college student or even as an adult?

WHAT YOU WANT TO SEE

Where would you like to go in your lifetime? What would you most like to see in your lifetime? List any top-of-mind ideas first, then progress to the questions below.

Early Years Dreams

When you were a little kid, did you have a favorite musical group you liked to jump and wiggle to? Does their music still appeal to you? Would you want to see them perform live?

Is there a place you spent a lot of time at as a young child that you have fond memories of but have not visited in a few years?

Was there a vacation destination you often asked to go to as a kid, but you have not been there yet?

Grade School Hopes

Did you ever learn about a place in school that you wished you could go to?

What would have been your dream vacation destination at this age?

Current Wishes

Who is your current favorite musician or group that you would love to see perform live?

What place would you like to travel to more than any other and what would you want to see or visit there?

WHO YOU WANT TO BE

What/who have you always wanted to be, whether it be a role you have wanted to fill or the type of person you have wanted to be (kind, outgoing, a leader)?

Early Years Dreams

What type of person did you play when you played make believe as a kid?

When you were little, what did you say when people asked you what you wanted to be when you grew up?

Who did you look up to most at a young age?

Grade School Hopes

Did your dream of what you would grow up to be change in grade school? What was it then?

Were there ever any roles—volunteering, work roles, or otherwise—you wished you could fill as a grade schooler, but you were too young at the time?

Current Wishes

What is your idea of your dream job when you grow up?

Are there any jobs or roles you would like to test out to see what they are like?

What do you hope younger kids will look up to you for, now and in the future?

WHO YOU WANT TO MEET

What person(s), living or dead, would you most like to hang out with (even briefly)?

Early Years Dreams

Who were your childhood heroes?

Did you ever think it would be interesting to ask a particular famous person about their life or their work?

Grade School Hopes

Name your favorite athlete, author, movie/tv star, and one other celebrity who stood out to you when you were in grade school.

Was there a person your age who achieved fame while you were in elementary school whom you thought you would like to meet?

Current Wishes

Who would you most like to meet right now?

Is there an individual whose shoes you would like to walk in for a day, or a certain person's way of living that you would like to try out?

Is there someone from your past who made an impression on you and you would like to reconnect with him or her?

Questions for Older Elementary (3rd through 5th Grade)

Think about your 3rd- through 5th-grader and their interests. No doubt they have some ideas of things they want to do, places they want to go, and people they want to meet. Encourage them to answer the questions below on their own. Have them answer only as many as they are comfortable with at the moment. Every day or two suggest answering a few more, reminding them that there are no right or wrong answers.

Resist the temptation to push the process. And be careful about requiring your child to answer the questions with you. For some kids this process moves more readily than for others. It is important that your child set the pace and not look at these questions as a chore.

If it will help a reluctant child, open a discussion about bucket lists by sharing over dinner one or two things you have discovered for your list. Express your enthusiasm for having lists you can all be working on.

WHAT YOU WANT TO DO

What is something that you have always wanted to do? Is there a sport you have wanted to try? A skill you have wanted to learn? Write down as many things as you can.

Younger Dreams

Remember when you were younger? What did you like to play most?

Was there something as a little kid that you wished you could do, but were too young to do then and never found a chance as you got older?

Current Wishes

What would be the most awesome way to spend a free day, if you had the money to do it and your parent(s) would let you?

Is there something you have been waiting to do, that now you might be old enough to try?

If you were told you could try something new without any problems, what new thing would you attempt?

Is there a pet you have always wanted to own, or an animal you have wanted to interact with?

Future Ideas

Is there something you would like to do when you are older – as a teenager or even as an adult?

WHAT YOU WANT TO SEE

What special places you would like to go to? How about a sports game or theatre performance you have always wanted to see? A museum or amusement park you have wanted to visit?

Younger Dreams

When you were a little kid, did you have a favorite musical group you liked to jump and wiggle to? Do you still like them enough to want to see them perform live?

Is there a place you spent a lot of time at as a young child that you have not been to a while and miss visiting?

When you were younger, did people talk about seeing something that made you want to see it too – a place or show or sport?

Current Wishes

Have you learned about a place in school that you wished you could visit yourself?

Who is your favorite musician or group that you would love to see perform live? If you are into a sport, is there a particular team or athlete you would like to see compete?

WHO YOU WANT TO BE

What have you always wanted to be? This could be a career you want to have or another role you would like to fill.

Younger Dreams

What type of person did you pretend to be when you played make believe as a kid?

When you were little, what did you say when people asked you what you wanted to be when you grew up?

Was there someone you really looked up to when you were younger?

Current Wishes

What would your dream job be?

Are you looking forward to playing a certain role – as a volunteer, in your school, or in your family— as you get older?

What do you hope younger kids will look up to you for, now and in the future?

WHO YOU WANT TO MEET

Can you think of any famous people you would like to hang out with, even briefly?

Younger Dreams

Who were your heroes when you were younger?

When you were little, did you ever think it would be fun to ask a certain famous person about their life or their work?

Current Wishes

Name your favorite athlete, author, movie/tv star and one other celebrity.

Is there a particular person who you would like to spend a day with to see what their life is like?

Questions to Ask
Preschoolers & Early Elementary

Read through the questions in this section with your child. To keep the interest of younger children, consider making it a game, where you take turns answering the question (although be careful that your answers do not lead them into mimicking what you have said instead of giving a heartfelt reply). You could ask them one question each night as you are tucking them into bed, keeping a notebook handy for recording the answers. Or you could go through a handful of questions over an after-school snack or at dinner, as if you were doing a rapid trivia game.

Consider your child's personality and which approach will work best. Or vary your approaches. Always follow your child's lead. If they are engaged and excited, you can keep going with questions longer than planned. But if they tire quickly, then put the questions aside for another day.

If your child is too young to write, encourage him to make pictures of his desires after you transfer them to the finished bucket list.

Note that some of the questions are less direct. These are there for you to capture your child's thinking at this age. You may be able to translate them into bucket list items now, or they may simply support an understanding of the child's heart-felt desires when reviewed at an older age.

If your child can't think of an answer or doesn't understand a question, skip it.

WHAT YOU WANT TO DO

What is something that you have always wanted to do, but have not gotten to yet?

Is there a sport you have been wanting to try? Something else you have wanted to learn how to do?

Is there an activity you would like to try out when you get older?

What would be your favorite way to spend a day if you got to choose everything you do?

Is there a pet you have always wanted to own, or an animal you have wanted to touch or see up close?

Is there something you would like to do when you are older – in grade school, as a teenager, or even as an adult?

WHAT YOU WANT TO SEE

What special place would you like to go to? How about a sports game or a show you want to see? Is there a museum or park you have wanted to visit?

Do you have some favorite music you like to jump and wiggle to? Would you like to see the musicians play it in real life?

WHO YOU WANT TO BE

Who have you always wanted to be like?

Who do you pretend to be when you play make believe?

What do you want to be when you grow up?

WHO YOU WANT TO MEET

Are there any famous people you would like to meet and talk to for a while?

Have you ever thought it would be interesting to ask a famous person about their life or their work? Who would you like to talk to?

Who is your favorite athlete, author, movie/tv star or other celebrity?

Creating Your Working Bucket List(s)

Phew! You have answered all the questions. Now comes the thrill of writing the list itself. View your bucket list as both an action plan and a list of possibilities and eventualities. The best way to make your dreams happen is to divide your ideas into three separate lists: short-term (in the next month to a year), near future (within the next three years), and future (whenever the pieces come together or the opportunity presents itself, possibly five, ten, even fifteen years down the road).

You may also want to create subheadings within your lists by purpose: do, see, be and meet, to help you find items quickly later when you refer back to your lists. Breaking down your list in this way also makes it easier to brainstorm and add new ideas as you cross items off your list.

Transfer your ideas as clearly defined objectives: for example, "I want to learn how to crochet" or "I would like to travel to the Grand Canyon" or "I have always wanted to meet Neil Diamond." To simplify the list you could write at the top: "I want to…" or a similar opening phrase.

If you are not sure whether you will be tackling an item now or in the distant future, place it on your short-term list. It will become clear once you put the lists to use whether an item makes sense as a short-term goal or not.

To guarantee you have included all the ideas on your list, highlight, cross out, or otherwise mark off the answers as they are transferred.

Your bucket list is an organic document. As you have grown and changed so have some of your desires (and you will find as you read some of your answers that you decide certain dreams no longer merit inclusion on the list at all). Once you have written up a starting bucket list, you will find some vague wishes will become more focused, while others that no longer appeal make way for more timely dreams.

Continue sifting and sorting your ideas over the course of a few days until you have either dumped or transferred all of them into one of the categories of your bucket list (broken down into short-term, near future and future). You will want to keep the process humming to prevent yourself from losing the excitement from the initial brainstorming. If you come across a dream from your past that you have already accomplished, put a circle around it or highlight it in a different color. We have a special purpose for those.

When you are done you should have one list broken down into three parts and a handful (or more!) of circled/highlighted items that you have already accomplished.

Have your teen/tween and older elementary children follow this same process. If they are open to your input, you could always guide them through the sorting, taking care to avoid judging or critiquing any of their answers.

Your insight into your child's personality and likes/dislikes could be a great assistance in parsing out some of the less obvious desires and dreams.

For younger children, talk them through their list creation. Their answers will be more direct and simpler to translate into a list. But they will still need your guidance in figuring out what they can expect to make happen in the next year and what may need to wait a while.

There! Your individual list is created. Are you getting excited about what you are going to do, see, be and meet? Great! Use that energy to create another compelling document: our shared family bucket list.

Creating a Shared Family Bucket List

As you created and discussed your individual bucket lists, did you find some dreams that you wanted to fulfill together, as a family? Perhaps some items overlapped on two or more lists. You might have recalled an adventure you want to recreate with your family. Maybe you came up with ideas of your own that you wished you could include on a child's list.

We have a place for those dreams. They go on a family bucket list.

Mom & Dad's Dreams For Before The Kids are Grown

We are going to develop this list by first having mom (and dad, if you are in a two-parent family) think through the four categories - do, see, be, and meet - within the framework of what you would like to accomplish before the kids are grown and have left your house.

If your children are all grown or nearly grown, your family bucket list may be only accomplished during holidays, vacations or other times when your family is all together. Or it may provide inspiration for gathering together more often.

Whatever your shape or situation as a family, you can still share a bucket list together. So list any items that came up on your individual lists that you would like to pursue as a family. Then consider the following questions to gain new ideas.

DO

Do you have any favorite traditions from your family of origin that you have not incorporated in your own family? Would it be worth trying them out once for the sake of sharing the experience with your children?

Is there a sport, hobby or other activity you want to teach your kids but you have not had time for, or the kids have not had the maturity for yet?

Name a type of food, dish, or restaurant you would like to introduce your children to.

SEE

Name the place about which you find yourself most often saying, "We should go there sometime."

Is there a museum, city, historical landmark, park or other location you have wanted to visit as a family? List as many as come to mind.

How about a performance or event that you would like your children to experience, whether theatre, sports competition, or musical group. What comes to mind?

Was there a movie that made a big impression on you in your formative years? If you'd like your children to view it too (at the appropriate time), add it to your list.

BE

Is there a value you cherish that you have been wanting to live out as a family that you could put into action together, such as serving the less fortunate, being hospitable by hosting an event, or giving up a family expense to show generosity through donating money saved?

MEET

Who could have an influence on the people your children become, whom you would like your children to talk with?

What person, who you have never met, embodies your family's personality or values most?

Family Bucket List Exercises
to Complete Together

Answer the following questions with everyone's input. You can do this over dinner or perhaps on a weekend night when you have plenty of time. Make joint family bucket listing into an event and serve up some fun food (maybe make it a pizza or appetizers night). Or tackle your list a few questions at a time over several nights or weekends. Whatever works for your busy family.

When you are ready to get started, lay down some ground rules such as:

- no interrupting when someone is talking

- no judging the answers verbally or by making faces or noises that register anything but enthusiasm

- consider every idea

- use consensus to create the final list (unless overruled by mom & dad who serve as the final authority on the list)

Take turns reading off the questions below or appoint someone to be the question reader. To make this into a game, you could create a question jar where you print the questions onto paper and then cut them into strips and fold them in half. Then take turns pulling out one question at a time to be answered, with one person serving as the secretary to collect the ideas onto one sheet of paper.

Answer as many questions as your family can in one sitting. If the ideas keep flowing, don't move on to another question until the momentum dies down.

If your children are slow to respond, share an idea or two from each category that you came up with yourself to get them started.

DO

Is there a new sport or activity we should all try together?

What skill would be valuable for all of us to learn together? Is there a skill we all have that we would like to improve?

When other people talk about our family, they think of us as the family that does... what? Is this the way we would like them to think of us? If not, how else do we want to be known?

Is there a tradition we have seen someone else keep that we would like to try in our family?

What type of vacation would we like to take (ski/cruise/beach, etc.) that we have never done before?

Do you have a restaurant or food you would like to check out?

SEE

In our next few big family vacations, what places would we like to try to visit?

Is there a show/group/sport that we should all attend together at least once before all the kids are grown?

What important object or work of art or document or artifact should we make a point of seeing first hand?

BE

Is there a role or position that we could all fill and have fun doing together? Is there somewhere you would like to try volunteering at as a family?

What character trait or virtue should we work at showing to the rest of the world?

Is there a tradition that we could share with other people on a regular basis – something that we would like to be known for?

MEET

What person would it be really cool for all of us to meet together?

Would anyone think it is really cool to meet our family?

Name someone famous (or not-so-famous) that you would like to not just meet, but spend some time talking with and get to know on a slightly personal level.

Is there a well-known person you would like spend time learning something from – a skill or the background behind a story or something else?

Compiling Your Family Bucket List

Follow the same process you used with the individual lists to compile your family list, making sure to merge Mom & Dad's list with your collective brainstorming. Remember to look at your family bucket list as both an action plan and a list of possibilities. The best way to make your dreams happen is to divide your ideas into three separate lists: short-term (in the next month to a year), near future (within the next three years), and future (whenever the pieces come together or the opportunity presents itself, possibly five, ten, even fifteen years in the future).

Depending on the ages of your children and how much you want to dedicate the list to things you will accomplish before your children leave your home, you may not have the third "future" category. But there may be things you hope to accomplish as a family after your kids leave home.

You may also want to create subheadings within your lists by purpose: do, see, be and meet, to help you find items quickly later when you refer back to your lists. Breaking down your list in this way, also makes it easier to brainstorm and add new ideas as you accomplish pieces of your list.

Transfer your ideas as clearly defined objectives: for example, "We want to learn how to golf as a family" or

"We would like to travel to Hawaii" or "We have always wanted to meet the President of the United States."

If you are not sure whether you will be tackling an item now or in the distant future, place it on your short-term list. It will become clear once you put the lists to use whether an item makes sense as a short-term goal or not.

To guarantee you have included all the ideas on your list, highlight, cross out, or otherwise mark off the answers as they are transferred.

Troubleshooting Your Family Bucket List

Taking into consideration the varying interests, ages and abilities of an entire family, particularly one with growing children, can be a challenge. This list, more than your individual lists, will likely require trial and error. Remember that you want to create an atmosphere of fun and adventure. If you are not getting a majority buy-in on the list or majority participation in accomplishing the list, this can't happen.

Here are some tips for troubleshooting some common problems:

Everyone can't seem to agree

You are looking for a majority consensus, not a unanimous vote. Initially this may be more of a challenge, particularly until the kids catch on to your vision. If every item on your joint list meets resistance from one corner or another, wait a few months to solidify the list while you allow your children to implement their individual lists. Let some excitement around the idea of bucket lists brew. Then try again as a family.

Too many choices make decisions difficult

You may also want to keep your initial family list short. Only include items that make everyone excited. If it means you cannot pursue anything on the shared list because the remaining ideas are too ambitious, point this out. Ask for creative solutions to help resolve the delay.

Cost concerns block progress

Be sure you have short-term goals that both cost money and can be done for free, so that finances will not cause a delay in taking action on list items. Future items may require savings. Therefore, why not get the kids involved in discussions about your family vacation or entertainment savings strategies? How would you like them to pitch in? Create a plan today for future goals and launch it. This will help everyone feel more involved in making the dream into a reality.

Make it a priority to complete one truly exciting dream from the family list, even if you all have to wait for it. If you get a big family dream (for example a trip to Disneyland) into the memory books, your commitment reinforces the idea that family bucket lists are fun and powerful.

Conflicting schedules get in the way

As kids get older, managing the family calendar may become more complex. You might find that the big getaway goal for your family just doesn't fit amongst other obligations. This is where you need to make sure you have appealing shorter-term ideas on your list. You may not be able to take a seven-day cruise, but I bet (for a lot less money) you could catch a cool concert in a city near your home.

Fitting in time to involve everyone might take planning six months to a year out. Yes, that is not ideal, but it gets your family where you want. Just be prepared to stick with your commitment when other opportunities arise down the road that conflict with your bucket list plans.

Age is an issue

Sometimes your family will want to tackle a project or outing or activity that does not match the ages of everyone in your family. When the opportunity to fulfill a bucket list wish presents itself, grab it with the understanding that this particular wish is age-appropriate and everyone in the family will get the chance when they reach the appropriate age.

Something comes up that was not already on the list

Guess what? Working through the questions in this book should only be a start to your bucket lists. In fact, you may find yourself noticing more and more activities and ideas to add to your family bucket list simply because you have put your list in place. Add away! Your list should only be bound by what sparks everyone's interest.

You decide against pursuing an idea on your list

Life changes, people change. A location that once seemed very appealing may have run down in the meantime. Or completing a similar pursuit may negate the desire to go after an item. Be willing to revise the list and delete ideas before completing them if they no longer interest your family or for some other reason no longer merit "bucket list" status. But as when you created the list, out of respect for everyone in your family, be sure to have a consensus on the removal.

Tips for Bucket List Living

Now that you have all of these lists, what are you going to do with them? Bucket list living is exciting, but maybe as you are reading all of these lists the only thing you are experiencing is anxiety over how you are going to execute all the amazing dreams your family has conceived.

Remember that bucket lists can last for a lifetime. If you feel pressured to hurry through making wishes happen, you may lose the joy that comes from dreaming and anticipating. So practice living with an "I don't know how we're going to make this happen, but we'll give it our best shot" attitude, instead of the "That's never going to happen" mindset.

Keep in mind that much of the fun your family can have with bucket lists comes in fleshing out and believing in your dreams—even when you are not quite sure how to make them all come true. Besides, putting each dream through the paces of what would need to come together for it to be fulfilled is a great exercise in creative thinking for the whole family. Maybe there are some steps you can take now, like research, comparison shopping, and calendar combining, even if the bucket list item itself won't come true for years. If so, go ahead and take those steps now and see what you learn.

Here are some tips on how to weave those dreams and desires into the fabric of family life:

Weekend Adventures & Close-to-home Experiences

Families that live out their bucket lists are always on the lookout for ways to incorporate their lists into downtime. This means keeping an eye on upcoming events in your community for chances to meet visiting authors, dignitaries and other celebrities. It means scoping out the nearby museums with traveling exhibits that could bring a rare item close to home. And it means rethinking your idea of what would be an ideal way to fulfill a dream. Consider what's possible as well as what's ideal.

Taking a hot air balloon ride is on my bucket list (as much as I am afraid of heights). However, in Illinois, where I live, this is not as popular of a sport as it is in more scenic regions of the country. The International Balloon Festival in Albuquerque, NM would be my choice of venues for a flight. But there also happens to be an annual balloon festival in the suburb next to ours, which we have attended almost every year for the past 10-plus years. There we have had a chance to watch balloon launches and landings (including unplanned landings in the field behind our house), chase balloons in a race, help pack up an envelope (the fabric part of the balloon), stand in a basket, and even climb inside an envelope inflated by blowing fans. Chances are, one of these years I will decide to go for it and take a ride in a balloon. In the meantime, I have been having loads of fun with all the other hot air balloon experiences.

Lessons, Clubs, Camps & Volunteer Opportunities

With park districts, YMCA programs and independent businesses offering larger and larger catalogs of classes, clubs and camps, it can feel like there is more to do than kids have time. But that same variety could be the passport to delving into one of those bucket list items.

The next time you are preparing to sign up for a class or camp, have your child look through the catalog with their bucket list in mind. Ask them if there is anything in the catalog that matches one of their dreams. You may need to translate the connection between some lessons or experiences and those dreams. For example, an opportunity to volunteer at a local humane society would be a great experience for a child hoping to grow up to be a veterinarian.

Also look at community college courses and adult offerings at park districts and community houses for ways to fulfill your own bucket list. You may even find parent-child classes where you can share the fun, such as the parent-child Irish Step Dance classes held in our city.

Birthdays & Other Gift Occasions

Another word for bucket list could be "wish list," which is also what we call the lists of gifts we would like to receive. With that in mind, you have a ready store of ideas for everyone in your family when it comes to gift-related holidays and birthdays. The trick here is not to hand over every item or experience they are hoping for, but to invest in dreams through the types of gifts you exchange.

You might want to give your child concert tickets to see that group he has been wanting to see. But you could also give him the group's latest album to demonstrate your appreciation of his love for their music. Or if your family plans to one day visit a foreign country, you could plant a seed for that dream by buying the Rosetta Stone language software as a joint holiday gift. Then "someday" won't seem so far off.

In our household, we have used gifts to encourage dreams in our children. Recently, after my eldest daughter expressed a desire to one day compete in the Olympics as a runner and had really rocked her first season on the junior high track team, we decided to buy her the track spikes she had been asking for. Then we wrapped them up and gave them to her for Christmas. That was her favorite gift, not only because she will enjoy using them in the upcoming track season, but also because it expressed our belief in her Olympic dreams.

Giving bucket list-related gifts is one way to incrementally move toward making those hopes come true. And it brings pieces of a long-off dream into the present.

School Breaks, Family Vacations & Detours

If your family is like most, time is your most valuable asset. You are probably already working hard and have little to spare. But spare time is a great time to tackle those bucket list wishes. The easiest place to find spare time is in what we already receive every year, namely school breaks and family vacations.

What do you do during your kids' breaks from school? Do you travel to visit family? Do you hunker down at home and just chill? Whatever you normally do, begin looking at how those vacation times can serve the individual and shared bucket lists you have created.

If you travel to visit family, consider whether your path might pass by a special destination on someone's list. Or think about whether it might be worth a slight detour to catch a once-in-a-lifetime event. This means looking ahead to the next break before you book your reservations or make any promises to friends or relatives.

Wherever you spend those breaks, consider whether there is an opportunity for a child (or mom or dad) to take a class or sit in on a lesson that they have marked on their list. Will there be a special person attending an event in that location or nearby, allowing you to schedule in a "meeting?" Check event listings on visitor bureau websites for the region you'll be traveling to. Or look at tour calendars on the websites of the celebrities you've decided you'd like to meet, to find whether your travel paths will intersect.

Likewise, when you sit down to plan your next family vacation, keep all of the bucket lists on hand. If you go to the same place each year because of a time-share or family vacation home, look for ways to enjoy a new bucket list activity at that location. If you're not bound to a particular location, instead of choosing the latest destination trending among your friends, consider trying out a hoped-for spot (and maybe invite some friends to join you for the adventure). You may learn during your vacation discussion that having the bucket lists visible prompts someone to remember an activity they had been hoping to try. With a little legwork you could give them the chance to experience during that vacation.

You may also create a destination-oriented family bucket list for every vacation destination. For example, one of our friends keeps track of interesting restaurants and must-try regional foods. Then he makes a point during his family vacations of visiting at least one of those restaurants or trying a new food such as: Skyline Chili in Cincinnati for their famous 4-way chili, meat-filled dough treats called "pasties" in the Upper Peninsula of Michigan, and any ice cream shop anyone has ever raved about. He will make a detour of even 50 miles to get to a spot if he has heard enough good things about it.

Likewise, my husband, an avid disc golfer (golf played with Frisbee-type flying discs), has the goal of playing as many disc golf courses in the U.S. as he can. So he carries a course directory with him on all of our vacations and attempts to play one each time we are away.

This approach to family vacations means being prepared to take the detours and suspend your itinerary when a bucket list opportunity presents itself. Keeping this spirit of spontaneity in the forefront of everyone's minds can change the tenor of every vacation to one of family adventure.

Unexpected Opportunities

Last year my husband, the disc golf fan, was elected to the position of Illinois State Coordinator for the Professional Disc Golf Association. Shortly after taking the role he received an invitation to play in the U.S. Disc Golf Championship. This elite tournament typically requires players to earn their spot by either playing on the professional circuit or by claiming a spot to represent their state through winning a specific qualifying tournament. My husband, much as he likes the sport, will likely never attain the level of play necessary to qualify for the championship. But this particular year, the championship planners decided to open the field to the state coordinators. We immediately recognized this bucket list opportunity. Soon we had lined up babysitters and time off work for the week of the tournament to take advantage of it.

Sometimes you won't be aware of a bucket list item until it presents itself. Part of the bucket list lifestyle is being prepared to say "yes" when a surprising once-in-a-lifetime opportunity arises. When you have a bucket list mentality, you will recognize opportunities like this when you see them. And you will already have buy-in from the rest of your family because they are invested in helping you realize your dreams as much as you have been helping them live out theirs. You will find it much easier to pull together your resources of time, money, and support once you have consistently seen the difference it makes to be fulfilling your longtime dreams in life as you go along.

Bucket List Celebrations & Records

One of the benefits of having a family bucket list is living a life that celebrates adventure. Part of your role in this as a parent is leading the charge in celebrating your family's accomplishments. And you can start the celebrating even before the first list has been inked. Here are some approaches to consider:

The Accomplishments List

When you created your individual lists I asked you to enumerate all of your past hopes and desires, even if you already lived them. Because they were accomplished already, you didn't put them on your official bucket list. So now go back and gather together all of those amazing events, meetings and experiences (that you either circled or highlighted when you created your original lists) into a separate list. Write them plain and simple. And if you remember any new accomplishments that did not come up in the exercises, write those down too.

Now read your list.

Are you getting fired up already? Isn't it amazing when you look back across the decades at how much you have seen and done? I am willing to bet there are items on that list that your children did not know about you. Your list should be both a source of celebration and inspiration. So what are you going to do with it?

You could put it in a folder or tuck it in a drawer. But if you are committed to a family bucket list lifestyle, then do something more with it. Print it out in a fancy font or use Wordle (www.wordle.net) to create a word cloud with your list. Then frame and hang it in a prominent spot in your home. Or gather some of the artifacts and souvenirs that represent your accomplishments and arrange them in a shadow box to showcase your amazing life thus far. Or document the stories behind the accomplishments, complete with photos. Put them in a special scrapbook or journal and record your stories to share with friends and family.

Celebrating the dreams you have already realized will set the stage for what your kids can expect when they realize their dreams. They will immediately see that a bucket list is not just about checking an item off. Nor is it about the joy of the particular experience alone. Bucket list living is an ongoing recognition of where we have been and where we are headed – together and alone – and the deep feelings we have experienced along the way.

Seventeen Ways To Record Bucket List Adventures

As you have just seen, part of the joy of bucket lists is reliving the stories of what has happened in our lives. And often it helps to have items that trigger our memories of these stories. After all, this is why we keep souvenirs from trips, weddings, and other special occasions. We know that when we see that special piece, it will bring to mind a memorable time – no matter how long ago it occurred.

Last year I started a SMASH™ Book of authors I have met. I went back into my photo archives and found pictures I had taken with famous writers I met. I pasted those into the pages of my book. I am also including each author's book cover images, along with notes about which of their books I most liked and why. In time, I will add stories about my meetings or association with these authors. Because of this SMASH book, I am much more intentional during book signings to get a photo of myself with the author, because I know it will make a great addition to my memory book.

So how will you commemorate your bucket lists going forward? One person might collect plates from places visited. Another may carry a special item in which he obtains autographs. Will you take photos along the way of both intermediate steps and ultimate goals reached? Do you plan to save a souvenir from each experience – ticket stubs, ribbons or medals won, key rings from places visited? Will you record the stories in some fashion – whether by video or in writing? Make sure to discuss these possibilities with your children. The earlier you start with tracking progress on a bucket list, the more valuable (and packed) your memory-keeper will become.

Until you've established a method of commemorating your bucket lists that suits you, you might think about purchasing a box and labeling it for memorabilia. This can work for any member of your family at any age. Buy a box for each person in the family. Then any souvenirs will have a safe home where they can be stored for future use.

Need more ideas? Here are eighteen ways to commemorate your bucket list adventure, after the fact:

1. Scrapbook

A scrapbook can be a good place to chronicle your adventures and catalog any paper mementos. Whether you make it fancy with decorative embellishments like scrapbook paper and stickers, or keep it simple with just photos and stories, a scrapbook allows you to showcase your adventures and your personality.

2. Shadow box

If you've gathered a variety of related objects and you want to exhibit them all together, you might want to consider a shadow box. This three-dimensional frame gives you space to tell a story with those objects. Then they can be put on display while being protected from damage. A series of shadow boxes can track your adventures over time or highlight various adventures taking place among the members of your family.

3. Journal

You don't have to be a writer to keep a journal. Simply jot down thoughts about your bucket list adventures – a word here, a phrase there, even a photo or two. Take it along on your adventures or pull it out afterwards. Journal on paper or keep a blog documenting your progress online.

4. Collection

Ticket stubs and theatre bills. Plates, thimbles, charms. Concert t-shirts. Postcards. If you like to bring home bits and pieces from your travels and bucket list events, you may find them taking a theme that comes together as a collection. Some people like to be intentional about purchasing a certain type of object in every place they travel or every event they attend. Watch your tastes and see if a unique item keeps coming home with you that you can eventually assemble into a collection to display.

5. Map

A large wall map pocked with pushpins can document your bucket list travels. But it can also note the places where memorable events occurred. If you like anchoring your stories on the sites where they took place, this could be a powerful visual for capturing your bucket list. Add a note beside each pin to describe what it stands for.

Google Maps has the capabilities for creating the same type of display in digital form. Simply generate a custom map, including digital photos (and even YouTube videos) using the "create map" button under "My Places" on maps.google.com.

6. Celebration Plate

What about having a special dinner plate you use to recognize the person who just completed a bucket list goal? You can buy a premade "Celebrate" or "You Are Special" plate. Or create your own using a plain ceramic plate and a Sharpie or other permanent Marker. With the marker, write the date and a short description on the plate. Then bake to set the ink (see full instructions here: www.fullofgreatideas.blogspot.com/2012/08/christmas-in-august-permanent-marker.html).

7. Pre-made Calendar

At the end of a calendar year you may decide to toss your regular wall calendar into your memento bin as an easy reference to what happened that year. Or you can buy a calendar that you keep separate and use only to record special events and adventures (and not for daily appointments and schedules).

8. Create Your Own Photo Calendar

To observe a year of adventures remembered, put together a photo calendar using an online photo service such as Shutterfly.com. Feature photos of favorite bucket list memories each month as inspiration for what you'll do throughout the year as you continue living the bucket list lifestyle.

9. Photobook

If you primarily record your accomplishments through photographs, you may want to consider compiling them in a photobook. Unlike a scrapbook, with many layers, lots of glue, and potentially delicate pieces, a printed photobook (from an Internet service such as Adoramapix.com) can provide you with a coffee-table quality book that highlights the images and stories of your adventures. The disadvantage of a photobook over a scrapbook is that the book needs to be completed before you can have it printed (and thus is not as accessible an option for an ongoing compilation). But the results can be impressive, making it worthwhile when you've accumulated a book-worth of memories. You can also keep an ongoing bucket list compilation through a series of photobooks.

10. Hat/shirt/canvas bag/autograph book

Remember autograph books? They still make them (just watch the crowds at Disney World to see children carrying Disney's commercial version). But you could designate any notebook or journal for capturing the signatures of noteworthy people you meet. Leave facing pages blank for inserting a photograph, if you'd like. Or you may prefer to be spontaneous and catch a signature on whatever you have with you at the moment, such as an article of clothing. Then you have the option of continuing to wear the item or display it on a wall (instead of your body).

11. Video journal, vlog, or montage

If you like to shoot video during special events – with a camera or a cell phone, then you may find yourself with a collection of memories in the shape of video footage. You could choose to post those online as a video log, where you can access them later. Or you might go through the different segments and edit them into a longer piece that highlights what you have done and seen, where you have been, and who you have met.

12. Quilt

Many fabric items (such as t-shirts and scarves) can be a challenge to display. Once you have finished wearing them, you could consider turning them into a quilt. Quilt squares can also contain shapes of images that represent pieces of your adventure. And technology even allows for the printing of photographs on fabric, which could be included in a quilt. If you do not have sewing skills, many professional quilters can transform your collection into a beautiful (and warm) bed- or wall-covering.

13. Slide show

For many years families commemorated events with slide shows. Technology has changed (something to keep in mind as you document your bucket list life), but the option still remains. Consider sharing your own slide show via a digital picture frame. You could add a sign or label to the edge of the frame stating "Bucket List" for guests to know the topic of the slide show. Then update the contents of the frame as you acquire new photos.

14. Memory jars

Using glass jars, you can contain and display tokens from your bucket list adventures. Try using a variety of shapes, sizes and colors (clear or opaque) to create interest within your display. For jars with wider mouths you can even insert a corresponding photo as a backdrop to the objects. If you like, create labels for the jars to mark the contents.

15. Curio cabinet or shelves

Whether you create one centralized location, such as a living room curio cabinet, or spread them throughout the house, consider offering each family member a shelf for displaying their bucket list souvenirs. You could even group shelves of different lengths and at different heights on a large wall to create an exhibit of what your family has been up to.

16. Photo Mosaic

If you have a large number of photos that are all meaningful to the story of your bucket list life, you could gather them together into a photo mosaic. Using online programs, such as Mozaiq (www.mozaiq.org) or PictoSaic (www.pictosaic.com) or even one of the mosaic creation apps like mymosaic, you upload a main photo. Then choose to use your own pictures or a selection of pre-made galleries for the tiny images. Order a print of the mosaic to display in your home.

17. Year-in-review letter

If your family follows the tradition of mailing an annual letter at the end of the year (often enclosed with Christmas cards), you probably already use that to document the highlights of your year – including bucket list accomplishments. Create a compendium of annual family letters as a record of your bucket list exploits. Or write a special version for your personal use that chronicles only what relates to your bucket lists. Then paste your year-in-review letter in an album or journal that can be read over and over.

18. Plastic storage container

You could choose to simply leave everything in a box, so the items can be taken out and handled, if this is what the list maker prefers. In this case, you may wish to use clear, see-through tubs, which invite more interaction than opaque boxes might. For future reference, you may want to tag each item, noting its significance so you can recall exactly where it is from and what it represents.

Whether you use one, two or many of these methods of commemorating your achievements, remember to enjoy the process. The way each member of your family chooses to share their story will be as individual as they are and as different as each of your bucket lists. Honor that individuality and encourage the expression of remembering. Celebrate those achievements together over and over again.

Conclusion:
Bucket List Living Changes Everything

By now I hope you have started writing up your bucket lists. And I hope you have caught a vision of what life will be like for your family as you live with each day holding the possibility of what others save for "someday." Choices about what to do, where to go, and how to spend your time will now be colored by the hope of reaching shared and individual goals. You will be living and repeating stories of what your written lists have brought about.

There is something about having a setting in which you can share your deepest desires and not just be accepted for them, but encouraged to bring them to life. Bucket list families receive the privilege of hosting a creative and co-creative environment for our children. As we let go of our hopes for our children and let them imagine their own future from their hearts, we give them greater chances at success. Kids learn to let their dreams lead instead of looking to us for instructions and goals. I hope you see your children's bucket lists as a catalyst for a life lived well and to the fullest. I hope your own dreams, whatever battering they may have taken over the course of your life, find the nurture and fruitfulness they deserve right in your own family.

Bucket lists germinated and grown in the context of family allow us to stretch and grow together. And with each successive adventure, we can become families who dare more, hope more, dream more. Together, moms, dads and kids living a bucket list lifestyle learn a resourcefulness that safe living could not teach us. We can experience our own strength and fearlessness that we might not otherwise discover living within the usual parameters of what has been expected of us. Living a bucket list life means living a life of family adventure, which sets the stage for a more adventurous life when kids grow up and move out on their own.

Your family's adventures await. Pick up your pen and get listing!

An Invitation to Connect:

I have created a Family Bucket Lists Facebook page for moms, dads and families who either want to live the bucket list lifestyle or who are already living it. This group is a place to share ideas on how to make dreams come true, connect dreams with intermediate steps, and encourage each other to fully live the adventure of the bucket list lifestyle. If you are on Facebook and would like to join us, you can find the group at: www.facebook.com/groups/160356867464143/

I have also created some bucket list boards on Pinterest, including one showcasing ways to commemorate your bucket list adventures. You can follow me there at: www.pinterest.com/amusingmomlara/

About the Author

Lara Krupicka has visited every stop on The Moscow Metro's famed Ring Line. But she still wants to eat her way across Tuscany. She has flown a Cessna Skyhawk single-engine airplane (with some assistance). But she has not yet learned how to fence. She has even swum with a sea turtle. Yet she is still waiting for the chance to meet actor Robin Williams.

Lara is a journalist and speaker with a passion for helping moms focus on what matters most in order to make confident choices for their lives. She specializes in topics that illustrate practical and meaningful decisions moms can make every day. Lara has been published in parenting magazines across the United States and Canada. She is a Toastmaster Competent Communicator and a member of the Redbud Writer's Guild.

Lara shares her bucket list dreams with her husband Mike and their three daughters. They launch their adventures from their home base in the suburbs of Chicago.

Acknowledgements

I am indebted to my husband, Mike, for letting me live my bucket list dream of growing up to be a writer. Every day is an adventure for me because of that. And I still have the fun of living out all those other dreams with you too.

Bethany, Katherine, and Evelyn, my three daughters, push me everyday to expand my idea of what is possible and what is enjoyable. I love being able to encourage their dreams. And I love sharing the bucket list life with them.

In my dream of being a writer I never expected to find such a great coach, teacher and editor as I have in Christina Katz. She always urges me to push toward the next goal. Without her, this book would still be a "someday" wish. I am so thankful to have connected with her and had the privilege to work with her.

I also recognize that I am incredibly fortunate to have the support and encouragement of fellow writers. All of you who have read my manuscripts have earned my deepest respect and gratitude. And I am honored that you trust me to partake in the adventure of writing with you.

And I am grateful to God, whom I believe places dreams and desires in each of our hearts that He is just waiting to bring to fruition so that He might delight in them with us. That I have any skill to write is due to His grace and His gifting.

Made in the USA
Coppell, TX
19 December 2019

13398612R00056